What's Under
That Rock

GREAT PLAINS   EASTERN

THIS IS A VERY SMALL TOAD - 1"-1½"

What's Under That Rock?

by

STEPHEN M. HOFFMAN

illustrated by Diane Dollar

ATHENEUM   1985   NEW YORK

To
my parents,
Sandy, Dr. Margaret Beeson,
and Pete Cohen.
You always knew I'd write this book.
Also,
thanks to Dr. Jim Johnson
and Joseph T. Collins
for their help.

Library of Congress Cataloging in Publication Data

Hoffman, Stephen A.
What's under that rock?

Bibliography.
Includes index.
SUMMARY: A field guide to the animals commonly
found under stones, logs, and objects resting on the
ground. Each animal's description is accompanied by
a map showing that animal's range within the United
States.
1. Animals—Identification—Juvenile literature.
2. Animals—Miscellanea—Juvenile literature.
[1. Animals—Identification.   2. Animals—Miscellanea]

I. Dollar, Diane, ill.   II. Title.
QL49.H675   1985   591   84-21643
ISBN 0-689-31081-1

TABLE OF CONTENTS

WHAT'S UNDER THAT ROCK?

Under every rock is a *microhabitat*. That word means "a small place where things live." And some very wild-looking wild animals can live under rocks no bigger than your hand. This book will help you identify many of the animals living in these small places.

These microhabitats are everywhere, not just under rocks. You can find them by turning over old boards, bricks, and other flat objects resting on the ground. Even an empty wading pool or garbage can usually has a community of tiny creatures underneath it.

The insects and other small animals in this book hide under things for several reasons.

Their tiny bodies lose water, or dehydrate, very quickly. If they lose too much water they will die. Fortunately, rocks trap moisture in the soil so it can't escape into the air. This dampness is perfect for preventing dehydration.

Shade is another reason animals live under things. The dark underside of a rock may be as much as 20 degrees Fahrenheit cooler than ground exposed to the sun's sizzling rays.

A third reason is the safe feeling animals get by crawling into tight spaces. You may have felt the same thing while hiding in a closet or a big cardboard box.

When you explore microhabitats, remember that animals don't all have the same habits. Some are active when the sun is up. Others are active when the sun is down.

Collared lizards, for example, hunt insects during the day, while narrow-mouth toads come out to look for bugs at night. Both may hide under the same rock but hardly ever at the same time.

Most of the animals you will meet under stones either die or hide deep in the ground as chilly winter weather approaches. So the best time of year to visit a microhabitat is during the warm months. Many of these creatures, you'll find, hide underground when it is hot and dry, too. They may only come to the surface after a heavy rain.

Look through this book before you go exploring. Get to know what sorts of things are found in your part of the country. The map that goes with each description of an animal will tell you where that animal is found. Naturally, they all won't live in your neighborhood. But a lot of them will, and the farther you get from "civilization," the more kinds you'll find.

Many creatures living in the country are never found in towns or cities. Salamanders, for instance, are very sensitive to water pollution. Ponds and streams in city parks may not seem dirty, but they are usually polluted enough to kill salamanders.

Exploring microhabitats doesn't call for much equipment. Many of the animals you find can be held in a jar while you identify them. A magnifying glass is nice for close-up viewing but is not something you'll have to have. Before you go too far, read carefully the "Words to Know" section of this book so you will understand what is meant when words such as "elytra" or "larvae" are used to describe an animal.

It's best not to pick up anything with your bare hands until you know it's safe to do so. Gloves will protect your fingers from nips or stings by critters like scorpions and spiders, and from being scraped by rough stones.

Gloves, however, will *not* protect you from rattlesnakes and other dangerous serpents. They can bite right through gloves. And a bite from one of these, even a baby, can be serious.

Some of the snakes in this book are poisonous, but you can identify them without getting too close. Unfortunately, the same kind of snake can come in many different patterns. It's possible to find a poisonous one that does not match any of the descrip-

tions in this book. Be safe and leave all snakes alone until you are certain which ones are harmless.

But don't worry too much about snakes. You won't see very many, and most of the ones you do find will be harmless. With these snakes, gloves are all that's needed to keep their sharp teeth from scratching your skin.

Also, many animals in this book, such as toads and salamanders, store bitter-tasting poisons in their bodies to keep from being eaten. When they are attacked by a hungry predator— or picked up by a person—these substances ooze out or are squirted at the attacker.

Such poisons can't hurt you unless they get in your eyes or mouth. Then they might make you sick or cause a painful burning sensation. Always wash your hands after touching any animal, but especially toads and salamanders.

You can make pets out of many of the things found under rocks. But try to resist the temptation to take home snakes, lizards, or salamanders. Many are difficult to keep alive and some are very rare. The rare ones should be left in the wild to breed. It might even be against the law in your state to catch them.

Finally, be considerate about lifting the "roof" off a microhabitat. Turn stones back over when you are done looking underneath. That way, the soil the stones protect won't dry out, and the animals depending on them for shelter won't have to find new hiding places.

And that's about all you need to know about exploring under rocks. Oh, there is one other thing. Whenever you take a walk, keep your eyes on the ground and remember to ask yourself, "What's under that rock?"

WORDS TO KNOW

abdomen (AB-duh-men)—that part of an insect's or spider's body behind the thorax; contains most of the internal organs.

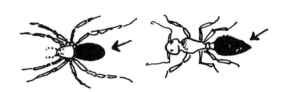

amphibian (am-FIB-ee-en)—frogs, toads, and salamanders; skin smooth or bumpy, not covered with scales; must lay their eggs in water or very damp places because the eggs don't have hard shells to keep them from drying out.

anal (A-null) **scale**—a large scale on the underside of snakes marking where the body ends and the tail begins; sometimes divided into two parts.

antennae (an-TEN-ee)—hairlike organs on the heads of most arthropods; used for smelling and tasting; also called "feelers."

arthropod (AR-thruh-pod)—an insect, scorpion, millipede, centipede, or other animal with six or more legs and a body divided into several parts.

cephalothorax (SEF-uh-lo-THOR-ax)—that part of a spider's body made up of the head and the thorax joined together.

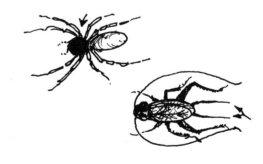

cerci (SIR-sigh)—a pair of fingerlike sense organs at the tip of the abdomens of many arthropods.

elytra (EL-i-truh)—the front pair of wings in beetles and many other insects; hardened into a protective shield covering the body; hind wings are folded underneath.

insect (IN-sect)—any arthropod that has three distinct body parts (head, thorax, and abdomen) plus six legs, and one pair of antennae; most have wings.

keeled (KEE-uld)—refers to snake or lizard scales that have a ridge like the keel on the bottom of a boat.

larvae (LAR-vee)—young amphibians or arthropods that have very different shapes and habits than their parents; as they grow older, larvae take on adult form and behavior.

pupil (PYOO-pull)—the black, center part of an animal's eye; pupils may be round or they may be narrow slits that are up and down (vertical) or side to side (horizontal).

reptile (REP-tile)—snakes, lizards, and turtles; reptiles have scales and lay leathery-shelled eggs that won't dry out on land.

segmented (SEG-men-ted)—divided into parts; insects, other arthropods, and earthworms have segmented bodies.

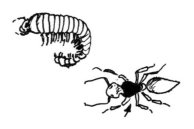

thorax (THOR-ax)—that part of an insect's body between the head and the abdomen; this is where the legs and wings are attached.

tubercle (TOO-burr-kull)—a horny knob on the hind feet of some kinds of toads; used for digging.

7

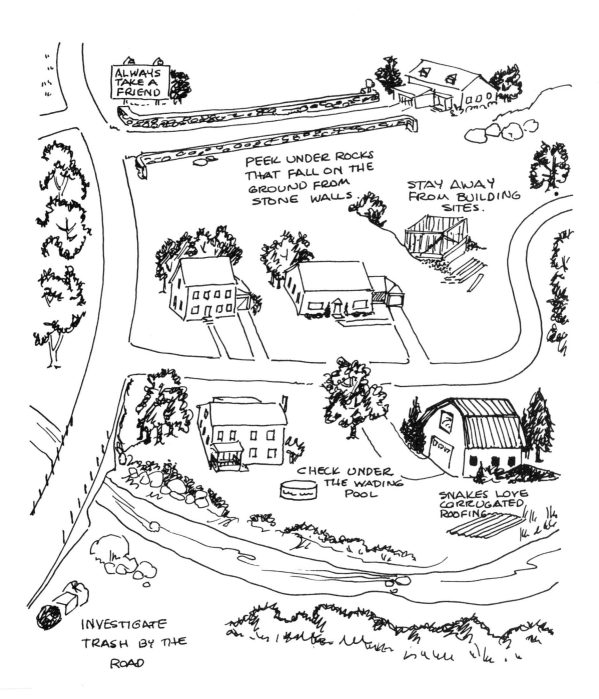

ALWAYS
TAKE A
FRIEND

PEEK UNDER ROCKS
THAT FALL ON THE
GROUND FROM
STONE WALLS.

STAY AWAY
FROM BUILDING
SITES.

CHECK UNDER
THE WADING
POOL

SNAKES LOVE
CORRUGATED
ROOFING

INVESTIGATE
TRASH BY THE
ROAD

8

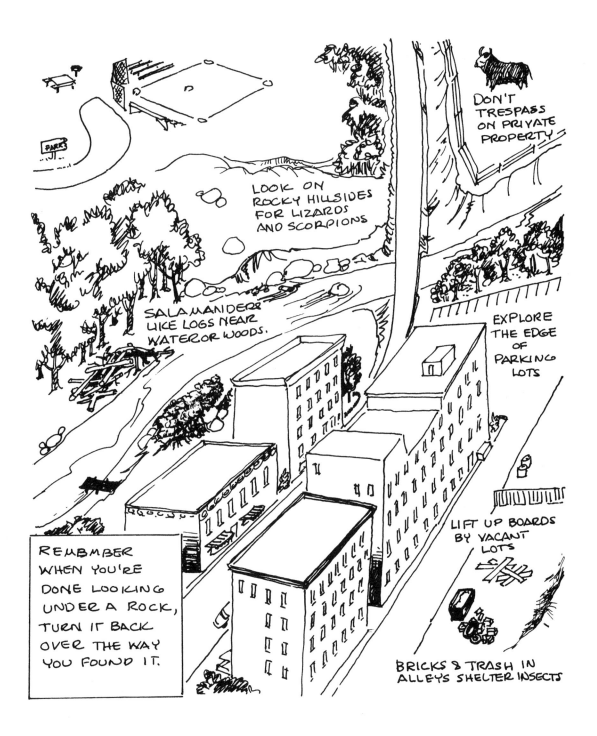

DON'T TRESPASS ON PRIVATE PROPERTY

LOOK ON ROCKY HILLSIDES FOR LIZARDS AND SCORPIONS

SALAMANDERS LIKE LOGS NEAR WATER OR WOODS.

EXPLORE THE EDGE OF PARKING LOTS

LIFT UP BOARDS BY VACANT LOTS

REMEMBER WHEN YOU'RE DONE LOOKING UNDER A ROCK, TURN IT BACK OVER THE WAY YOU FOUND IT.

BRICKS & TRASH IN ALLEYS SHELTER INSECTS

9

Mollusks & Segmented Worms

SNAILS AND SLUGS

DESCRIPTION: The difference between snails and slugs is the cone-shaped or disk-shaped shell a snail carries on its back. Slugs are just types of snails that don't have shells.

Both animals have long, soft bodies that can stretch as if made of rubber. They have a blunt tail in back and 2 pairs of fingerlike tentacles on the head. The first pair is for smelling and tasting, like the antennae of an insect. The second pair has an eye at the tip of each tentacle. What looks like the belly is actually called the "foot."

The skin of these creatures is bumpy and wet and may be white, yellow, brown, gray, or black. Snail shells are generally yellow, light tan, or dark brown. Sometimes they are decorated with darker spots or stripes.

A snail's shell, which grows as its owner does, may be ⅛ to 1 inch long. Young look just like adults, only smaller.

HABITS: Slugs and snails are mollusks (MOLL-usks). This group of animals includes clams, oysters, squids, and octopuses.

You never have to worry about catching them because their top speed is only 10 or 12 feet per hour. As they move around, they leave glistening trails of slime that protect their undersides from twigs and stones. This slippery substance oozes from a gland on the foot, just behind the mouth.

In dry months, you may find shells that are glued to the underside of rocks and other objects. The snails inside them are waiting until it rains again. By sealing their shells tightly against a solid surface, they can prevent the tiny amount of water in their bodies from evaporating. Snails can stay like this for months, if necessary.

Most slugs and snails are plant eaters. They scrape off bits of food from leaves and stems with their rasp-like tongues. They can be very serious garden pests. A few kinds hunt down and attack other snails and slugs, as well as earthworms.

Like earthworms (p. 14), these mollusks are both male and female. But to lay eggs, they must find mates. However, snails and slugs cannot breed with each other, even though they are closely related.

In summer, those animals that have mated dig shallow burrows under logs and other ground cover. They lay a few or as many as 40 eggs at the bottom of these holes. The eggs hatch after about one month.

EYE

EYE

SNAIL

EYES

SLUG

EARTHWORMS

DESCRIPTION: Earthworms look like small snakes, although they are not related to reptiles. Most are grayish-pink to dark tan. All are coated with slime.

A worm's body is divided into dozens of ringlike segments. There are 4 pairs of tiny hairs, or setae (SET-ee), on all but the first and last segments. You can feel these setae as a worm slides through your fingers. On the back is a wide band called the clitellum (kly-TELL-um). It is closest to the worm's front end, where there is only a small mouth.

Adults are 4 to 12 inches long. Young are smaller and don't have clitellums.

Don't confuse worms with worm snakes (p. 74). Worm snakes have eyes, nostrils, and scaly skin. They are smooth and shiny but not wet. Earthworms don't have scales or any features other than a mouth, and their bodies are segmented.

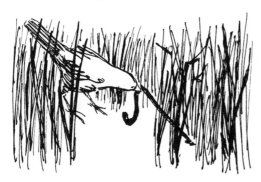

HABITS: Worms are completely harmless. Their only defense when grabbed is to hang on and pull the other way. Their setae act as anchors to hold them firmly in the ground. So firmly, in fact, that sometimes a bird—or a fisherman looking for bait—only gets part of a worm. When this happens, the other part slides back underground and eventually regrows much of the missing portion.

Food is any decaying plant or animal matter. At night, worms stretch out of their burrows, grab dead leaves with their tiny mouths, and pull them underground so they can eat in safety.

They also swallow dirt, digesting the decayed matter it contains and expelling the rest. As the dirt passes through their bodies, it is mixed with minerals that plants need. In this way, worms fertilize the soil.

Worms breed almost all year long, but especially during warm, wet weather. Every worm is both male and female. Yet each must find a mate before it can produce young.

After mating, worms lay 4 to 20 eggs inside lemon-shaped capsules, which they form out of thick slime. The eggs hatch in two to three weeks. The babies eat through the capsules, then burrow away on their own.

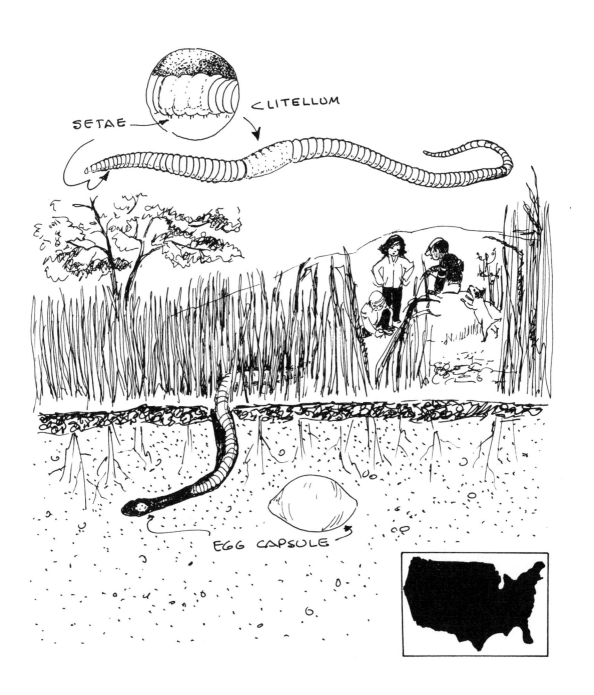

SETAE

CLITELLUM

EGG CAPSULE

Arthropods

17

ANTS AND TERMITES

DESCRIPTION: People often get ants and termites confused, but it's easy to tell them apart. Ants are shiny black, brown, yellowish-brown, or reddish-orange. Sometimes they have two colors but usually just one. The abdomen is pinched in the middle, which gives ants a very slender look.

Termites are white or nearly so, sometimes with shiny tan heads. Their soft, lumpy bodies are not pinched.

Both insects are generally less than ¼ inch long, but a few kinds of ants are twice this length.

HABITS: Termites are not related to ants, even though they are often called "white ants." Their closest living relatives are actually the roaches (p. 26).

Most people know that termites eat wood. But not all termites live inside the wood they eat. Many kinds build their homes in the soil and dig tunnels to nearby logs, wooden fence posts, or dead trees.

Ants don't eat wood but many kinds like plant sap, seeds, or leaves. Others prefer live insects and decaying animal matter.

Most ants bite and many can sting. Termites can't sting but the big-headed soldiers have large jaws, which they use to defend the colony.

Ants and termites often start nests underneath large rocks to protect the new colonies from predators and bad weather. Some colonies have barely a dozen members while others might have hundreds or even thousands.

When you find an ant or termite nest, you may see a few insects with wings. These are not queens. Think of them as princes and princesses. They are special adults—royal children—that one day will leave their nest to start new colonies.

Every spring and summer, all of the royal children from hundreds of nearby nests take to the air at the same time. They swarm through the sky in great clouds until they find mates. Then each pair drops to the ground and searches for a safe hiding place where the female can begin laying eggs. But before settling down, the adults twist and tug at their long wings until they break off.

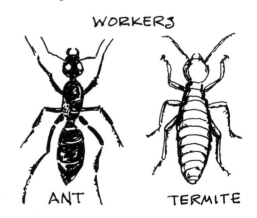

WORKERS

ANT   TERMITE

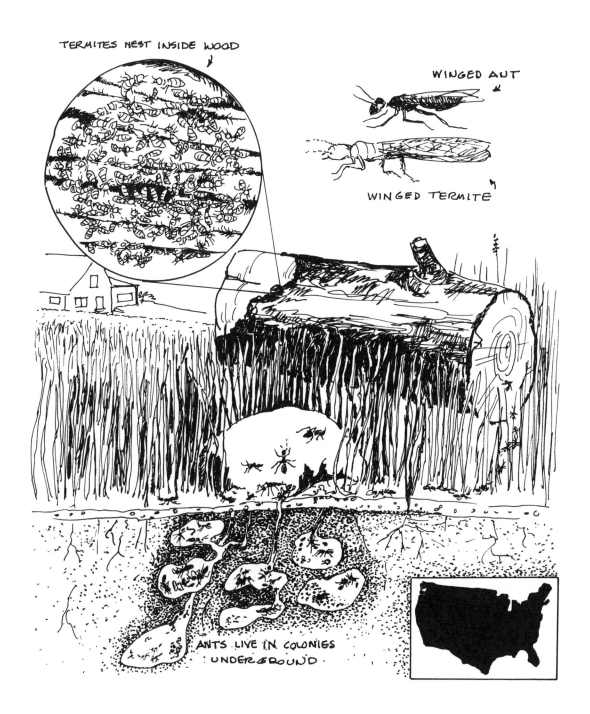

TERMITES NEST INSIDE WOOD

WINGED ANT

WINGED TERMITE

ANTS LIVE IN COLONIES UNDERGROUND

19

GROUND AND DARKLING BEETLES

DESCRIPTION: Ground beetles are ½ to 1 inch long and oval or oblong in shape. They are usually shiny black or brown, but can also be yellow, blue, green, or purple. Grooves and rows of dents decorate their elytra. Sometimes the elytra are one color in the middle and another color around the edges.

A ground beetle's head is narrower than its thorax, and the thorax is narrower than the abdomen.

Darkling beetles are similar to ground beetles. You can tell the difference by turning them over and looking at their legs. Ground beetles are the *only* rock-dwelling insects that have hind legs like those illustrated at right.

HABITS: Most kinds of ground beetles are found in the eastern half of the United States and are very common. They often fly to lights at night, but almost never use their wings to escape danger. Instead, they run quickly for cover when disturbed.

One kind, called the bombardier beetle, can squirt out chemicals from the tip of its abdomen. These explode with a pop and a puff of steam when they touch the air. The tiny explosions are harmless. But they can startle a hungry predator long enough for the bombardier to scramble safely away.

Bombardier beetles have bluish-black elytra and yellowish front legs, head, and thorax.

Almost all darkling beetles live in the western half of the United States, especially in desert areas. They come to porch lights during warm weather, too.

The darkling beetles known as *Eleodes* (ee-LOY-deez) are easy to identify by the way they run from danger. They hold their rear ends high in the air as if getting ready to do head stands. Pick one up and a harmless but smelly black fluid will ooze from its abdomen.

Most ground beetles are hunters, chasing after insects and spiders at night. The shiny, emerald green *Calosoma* (cal-uh-SO-muh), for instance, is called the caterpillar hunter. It often climbs into low bushes to search for moth and butterfly larvae.

Darkling beetles, on the other hand, are plant eaters. They attack leaves, bark, seeds, and fungus.

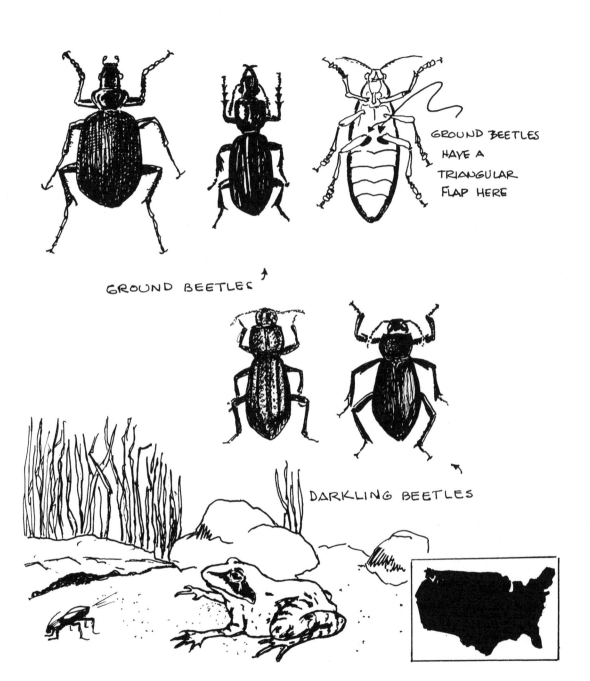

GROUND BEETLES HAVE A TRIANGULAR FLAP HERE

GROUND BEETLES

DARKLING BEETLES

21

CRICKETS

DESCRIPTION: Crickets look like fat grasshoppers ½ to 1 inch long. They are shiny brown or black, with thread-like antennae and large hind legs for jumping. All crickets carry a pair of stubby cerci, but only females have an egg-laying tube, or ovipositor (O-vi-POZ-i-ter), as well.

HABITS: Crickets, like their grasshopper relatives, can quickly hop away from danger. You've got to be fast to catch them.

If you'd like to hear one chirp up close, remember that males are better musicians than females. They chirp to attract mates and frighten away other males. A cricket "sings" by rubbing its wings together. As one edge is drawn across the other, it causes a high-pitched squeak or chirp.

After mating with a musical male, a female pushes her ovipositor into the ground and squeezes out eggs.

Crickets usually eat green plants, but they aren't considered pests. House crickets sometimes do become pests by moving indoors to escape the cold as fall approaches. They nibble paper, cloth, and anything else containing starch.

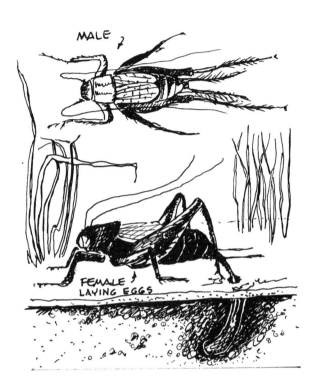

MALE

FEMALE
LAYING EGGS

ROVE BEETLES

DESCRIPTION: Rove beetles, less than ¾ inch long, have very short elytra. So short, in fact, their abdomens are almost completely uncovered. Their sharp, curved jaws point forward and are so long they cross.

Most of these insects are dull black or brown, but some wear bright colors.

When frightened, rove beetles bend their abdomens upward as if to sting. This is a good way to identify them.

Earwigs (p. 25) are easily mistaken for rove beetles because they have short elytra, too. But earwigs have pincers at their rear ends and they don't arch their bodies when alarmed.

HABITS: Don't be fooled when this beetle goes into its body-bending act. This is just a trick to make you think it can sting. None of them can, but some will bite painfully if you pick them up barehanded. Catching them isn't easy, though. They are fast on their feet and also very good fliers.

Most rove beetles eat insects. Their long legs come in handy for chasing after prey. A few kinds prefer decaying plants and animals.

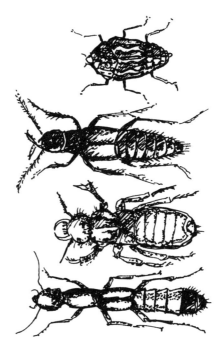

THESE ARE JUST A FEW KINDS OF ROVE BEETLES

WHITE GRUBS

DESCRIPTION: White grubs may not look like insects, but they are the larvae of scarab beetles. They have shiny brown heads and soft, lumpy, yellowish-white bodies. Their 6 short legs are crowded together at the front end. Some grubs grow to be as long as 1½ inches before turning into adults.

The adult scarab beetles are not usually found under rocks.

HABITS: When you find a grub, it will probably be curled into a doughnut shape in a small space it has made in the soil. They hardly move except to curl up even more when disturbed. Scarab larvae may spend as many as three years underground before they are ready to become adults and push up to the surface.

White grubs usually eat plant roots. They can cause a lot of damage to lawns, golf courses, and crops. Adult scarabs, such as Japanese and June beetles, feed on the above-ground parts of many trees and flowers. Most of the beetles attracted to porch lights during spring and summer are scarabs.

EARWIGS

DESCRIPTION: Earwigs are narrow, flat insects ¼ to 1 inch long. Their very short elytra reveal most of the abdomen. The end of the abdomen is equipped with large pincerlike cerci. Females usually have straight pincers. Males have curved. Earwigs are brownish or black.

They can be confused with rove beetles (p. 23), which also have short elytra. But rove beetles don't have pincers.

HABITS: The earwig got its name because people used to believe these insects crawled into the ears of sleeping humans. This isn't true, but earwigs do come out at night to feed on decaying plants and animals.

Unlike most insects, earwigs use their cerci for defense. Careful! Some can give a painful nip. When disturbed, a few kinds can squirt a bad-smelling fluid from tiny holes along their abdomens.

After mating, females lay their eggs in burrows they dig. They stand guard until the eggs hatch.

The European earwig, pictured here, is very common in the United States.

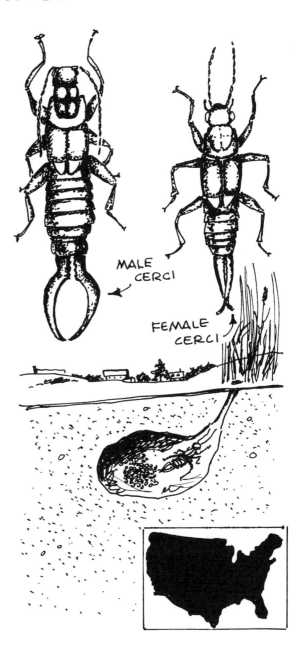

MALE CERCI

FEMALE CERCI

25

ROACHES

DESCRIPTION: Roaches are flat, oval, shiny black or brown insects. They have 2 fingerlike cerci at the rear end, but these may be hidden by the wings. Their antennae are long, slender threads. Seen from above, a roach's head may be hidden under its thorax.

Adults are about 1 to 1½ inches long. Young resemble their parents.

The wood roach is a common outdoor variety. Its oval thorax is light around the edges and dark in the middle. Other kinds of roaches have more triangular thoraxes.

HABITS: Roaches that live indoors almost never fly, even though they have large wings. Their main defense against danger is to run. Wood roaches are not only fast on their feet, but they are excellent fliers, too. They often fly to porch lights on warm evenings.

Wood roaches will eat almost any kind of rotting plant or animal matter. Unlike other roaches, they usually don't become indoor pests.

Instead of laying their eggs one at a time the way most insects do, roaches keep theirs all together in papery, brown capsules. The females of some kinds attach these containers to the ends of their abdomens and carry them around until the eggs inside hatch.

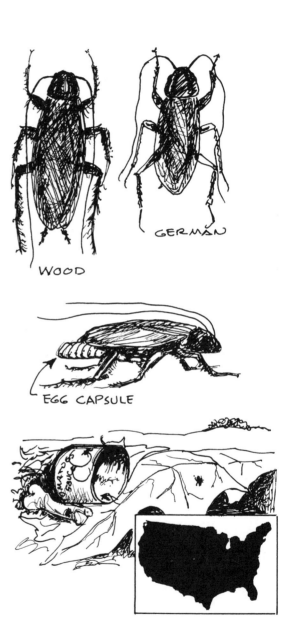

WOOD

GERMAN

EGG CAPSULE

26

SOW BUGS

DESCRIPTION: Sow bugs are about ½ inch long, curved on top and longer than they are wide—like tiny watermelons cut in half the long way. Seven pairs of legs and a pair of antennae peek out from under their black, gray, or brown shells. Young look just like adults, only smaller.

HABITS: Sow bugs aren't really bugs at all. They're crustaceans (krus-TAY-shuns), a group of animals that includes lobsters, shrimp, and barnacles. People often call them pillbugs and roly-polys because some kinds roll into little pill-sized balls when picked up. This is their only defense.

Even though they live on land, sow bugs breathe through gills, just as their ocean-dwelling cousins do. The little crustacean's gills are located on its underside. They have to be wet to work, so you'll only find sow bugs where there is plenty of moisture.

Sow bugs mostly eat decaying plants, but sometimes they become garden pests by attacking young seedlings.

Females that have mated carry their developing eggs in a tiny pocket on their undersides. This pocket is called a brood pouch.

WOLF SPIDERS

DESCRIPTION: Wolf spiders are probably the largest spiders you'll find under a rock. Some may have bodies as long as 1¼ inches. But many kinds are smaller.

They range in color from light gray to dark brown and black, including their hairy legs. A light pattern runs down the middle of the spider's body. This might be a complicated design with yellow or white spots and bars, or just a simple stripe, depending on the kind of spider.

Wolf spiders have 8 dark eyes arranged in 3 rows. The bottom row has 4 small eyes. The middle row has 2 very large eyes. Two smaller eyes are in the top row. Most other spiders have eyes set in only 2 rows.

HABITS: These long-legged hunters aren't dangerous, except to insects. Large ones, however, can give you a painful bite. Like the jumping spiders, wolf spiders don't build sticky webs for catching food. Instead, wolf spiders chase their prey across the ground just as real wolves run after larger animals.

After mating in the springtime, females lay their eggs on a sheet of silk and wrap them up. They carry the grayish, round egg sac by gluing it to their abdomens with a drop of silk. Upon hatching, the spiderlings scramble up their mother's legs and ride on her back for many days. Eventually, they fall off and must survive without her protection.

You can often find these spiders hiding in silk shelters they spin beneath rocks. This is about the only home a wolf spider ever makes.

Wolf spiders are easy to keep as pets if given crickets, mealworms, or other live insects for food. Provide a small jar lid with a few drops of water because they need to drink. Don't put two spiders together or one will eat the other.

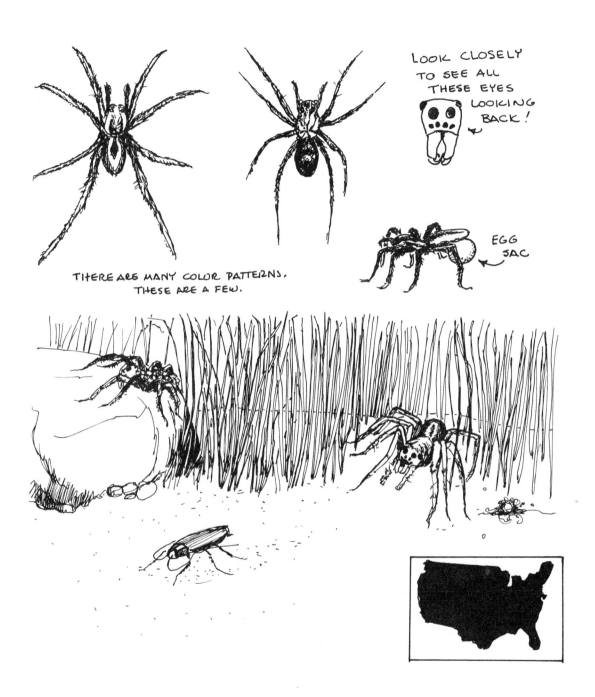

LOOK CLOSELY TO SEE ALL THESE EYES LOOKING BACK!

THERE ARE MANY COLOR PATTERNS. THESE ARE A FEW.

EGG SAC

JUMPING SPIDERS

DESCRIPTION: Jumping spiders look like tiny weight lifters that are less than ½ inch long. They have a muscular appearance because their front legs are usually thicker than the others.

If you can get close enough, the best way to identify them is by their 6 eyes. These are arranged in 3 rows, with a pair of eyes in each row. The bottom eyes are so much larger than the others, they stick out like the headlights on a car.

A common kind of jumping spider found under stones and boards is called *Phidippus* (FID-uh-pis). *Phidippus* is usually black with white, yellow, or orange spots on its abdomen. Males have large green jaws that sparkle in the sun like emeralds.

HABITS: Instead of catching insects in webs the way other spiders do, jumping spiders wander around until they spot a victim. Then they pounce on it, holding it tightly in their strong front legs. They can leap many times their own length.

Those large eyes are a big help when hunting. Without sharp vision to guide them, these broad jump champions could never land exactly on top of their prey.

You can often find jumping spiders at night, sleeping under silk sheets they attach to the underside of their hiding places. They also hibernate in these shelters, so you might see them in the winter when most other creatures that live under rocks have disappeared.

When a male jumping spider finds a female, he signals to her by waving his front legs, wagging his abdomen, and hopping. If the female is willing to mate with him, she waves back. Females that have mated build silk cocoons for their eggs, then stand guard until the eggs hatch.

ALWAYS PUT ROCKS BACK THE WAY YOU FIND THEM.

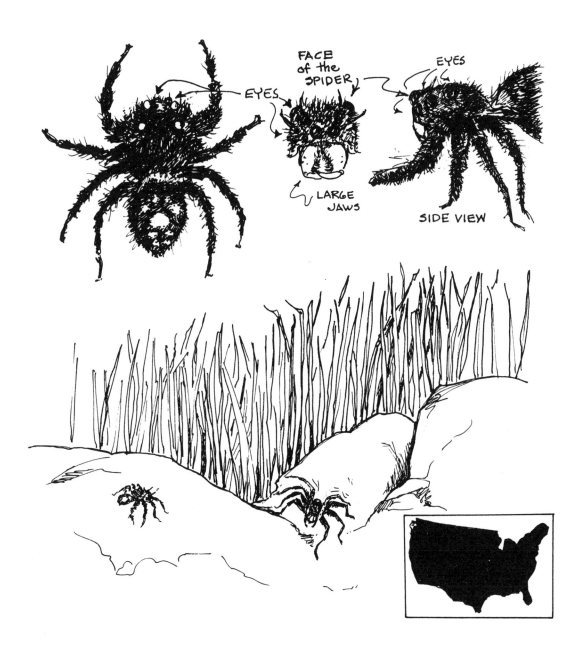

EYES

FACE
of the
SPIDER

EYES

LARGE
JAWS

SIDE VIEW

HARVEST MITES

DESCRIPTION: Harvest mites look like fat, orange spiders with ¼-inch-long bodies. Like spiders, they have 8 legs. But it is easy to tell these two arthropods apart.

Spiders have a "waist" where cephalothorax and abdomen come together. It looks as if they are wearing belts that are pulled too tight. Mites don't have this narrow look. Harvest-men (p. 33) don't either, but their legs are much longer and thinner than a mite's.

HABITS: Adults are completely harmless. You needn't worry about picking one up. They eat small insects and insect eggs.

Young mites are another matter. These are the tiny, red chiggers that help themselves to a free meal from you or any other animal walking through tall, wet grass. Chiggers can leave you itching for days after they bite.

Mated female mites lay their eggs on plants. After hatching, the larvae crawl up the plant stems and wait for animals to wander by.

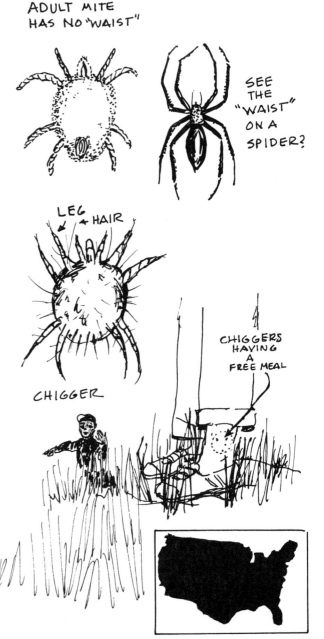

ADULT MITE HAS NO "WAIST"

SEE THE "WAIST" ON A SPIDER?

LEG HAIR

CHIGGER

CHIGGERS HAVING A FREE MEAL

HARVESTMEN

DESCRIPTION: Harvestmen, or daddy longlegs, are easily identified by their 8 incredibly long, threadlike legs. From head to tip of abdomen, they are barely ¼ inch long. But their legs may stretch 4 or 5 inches from end to end. Harvestmen are usually pale to dark brown.

These animals are not spiders. Their oval bodies aren't divided into two parts as a spider's body is.

HABITS: Daddy longlegs can be handled without fear. Some kinds squirt themselves with a smelly fluid when disturbed. This keeps many hungry predators from eating them. But it won't hurt you. These arthropods do not bite.

Harvestmen are common in most parts of the country. They feed on plant juices and dead insects. Some hunt live insects, too.

As autumn approaches, mated females lay their eggs under stones, in the ground, or in the cracks of old wood.

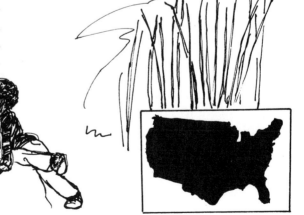

SPIDERS HAVE A "WAIST"

NO "WAIST"

33

BROWN RECLUSE SPIDERS

DESCRIPTION: The poisonous brown recluse (REK-loose) spider is actually yellowish-brown, and less than ½ inch long. A dark violin-shaped mark on its cephalothorax gives the recluse its other name, violin spider.

HABITS: The recluse builds a small tangle of silken threads beneath stones, logs, and other ground cover. It eats insects, smaller spiders, and anything else that stumbles into this snare.

Unlike most spiders, the brown recluse is dangerous to humans. Never pick one up. A person who's been bitten may not even know it until hours later when the bite becomes red and tender. Within a day, a blister forms and the victim may have chills, fever, and feel very sick. The wound takes a long time to heal, but very few people have ever died from the brown recluse's poison.

Females that have mated will lay their eggs anytime during the year, as long as it's warm. The eggs are sealed inside flattened, round sacs, which the spiders attach to their webs. These sacs are often longer than the females that spin them.

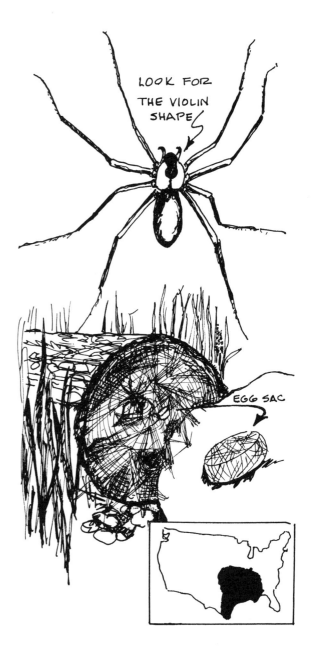

LOOK FOR THE VIOLIN SHAPE

EGG SAC

SCORPIONS

DESCRIPTION: Scorpions have 8 legs, a long tail, and 2 large pincers held out in front on "arms." Most are 2 or 3 inches long from head to tip of tail. They are pale brown, yellow, or gray, and as flat as if run over by a steamroller.

Scorpions are not insects, but something entirely different.

HABITS: If you were a dinosaur living today, scorpions would be one of the few animals you would recognize from the past. Fossil scorpions that are 25 million years old look almost exactly like their modern relatives. These creatures were among the first animals to live on land.

Scorpions carry a stinger at the tip of their flexible tails, so don't pick them up with your bare fingers. The poison of most kinds causes nothing worse than mild pain, like a bee sting. But two types of scorpions are very dangerous to humans. Both live only in the state of Arizona.

Although they will sting in self-defense, scorpions mostly use their poison to kill the spiders and small insects they eat.

Adults perform a mating dance by holding onto each other's pincers and whirling around and around. Babies are born alive in early summer and look just like their parents. They ride on their mother's back for about a week before wandering away to survive on their own.

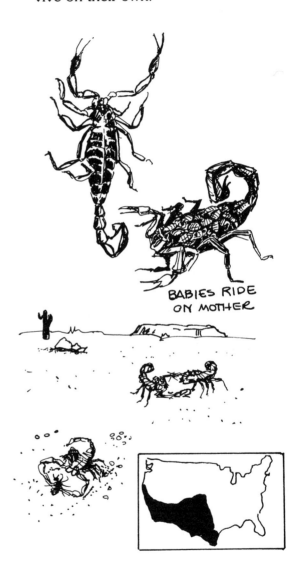

BABIES RIDE ON MOTHER

MILLIPEDES AND CENTIPEDES

DESCRIPTION: Millipedes and centipedes look alike, but these arthropods are very different from each other.

Millipedes are round and thin, like short pieces of spaghetti. Their flexible bodies are divided into segments. Each segment has 2 pairs of tiny legs that curl underneath the millipede. Adults have about 30 segments, but babies hatch with only a few. They add new segments as they grow older.

Most millipedes are dull brown, black, or dark gray and less than 2 inches long.

Centipedes are similar to millipedes, only flatter. Each body segment has a *single* pair of *long* legs sticking out to the sides. The last pair points backward. It looks so much like the antennae that when a centipede stands still, it's hard to tell which end is the front.

Centipedes are usually reddish-orange or gray and may be up to 6 inches long.

HABITS: One of the best ways to tell these two arthropods apart is by the way they move. Centipedes are very fast and run with a snaky, side-to-side wiggle. Millipedes are quite slow and don't wiggle as they move.

Be careful about picking up these lookalikes until you can tell the difference. Centipedes have a pair of poisonous claws hidden beneath their heads. Even though they aren't dangerous to humans, some can give a painful sting.

Millipedes are completely harmless, often curling up and playing dead when touched. Many kinds give off a bad-smelling fluid, too. This substance can't hurt people, but sometimes it is strong enough to kill insects kept in a jar with millipedes.

Millipedes eat decaying plants. Centipedes are hunters, using their poisonous claws to kill spiders, insects, and earthworms.

After mating in the summer, females of both of these arthropods lay eggs in damp places. Some kinds of millipedes dig underground nests. Others scatter their eggs as they move about, leaving one here and one there. Centipedes leave their eggs in many different places, too.

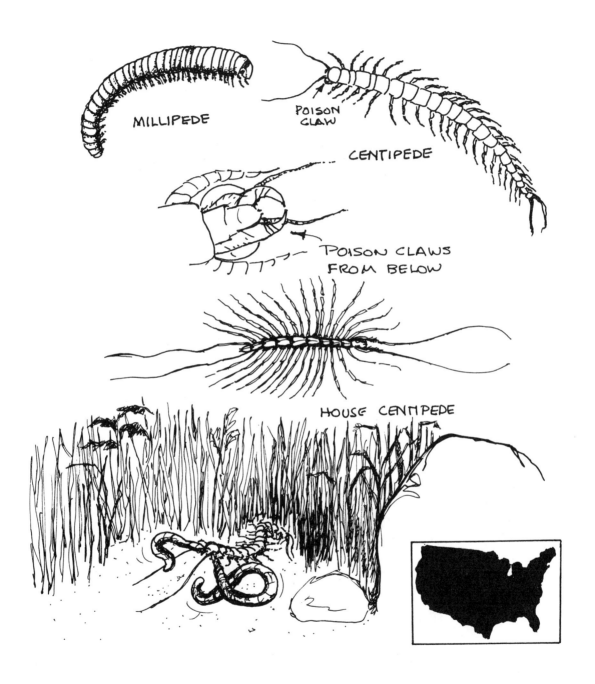

MILLIPEDE

POISON CLAW

CENTIPEDE

POISON CLAWS FROM BELOW

HOUSE CENTIPEDE

Amphibians

BROOK SALAMANDERS

DESCRIPTION: Brook salamanders are nearly always yellow or yellow-orange, with dark brown stripes or spots. Sometimes they are peppered with black specks.

Three kinds of brook salamanders are common under rocks and other ground cover.

The two-lined variety has a stripe on each side of the back and tail, starting at the eye. These stripes often break up into blotches on the tail.

Three-lined brook salamanders look like their two-lined cousins but have a third stripe down the middle of the back. This middle stripe is much narrower than the side stripes.

The long-tailed brook salamander is the only yellowish salamander with vertical black markings on its tail. Instead of stripes, it has dark spots along its back and sides. An adult's tail is much longer than its head and body together. Young ones have shorter tails.

Adult brook salamanders are 2 to 6 inches long. Mature males often have a fingerlike growth hanging down from the top of each nostril.

HABITS: These amphibians stick close to brooks and quiet ponds. But on rainy or humid nights they may wander far into the surrounding countryside. Come sunup, they take shelter under rocks and logs. They also are found near cave openings.

Their diet includes aquatic insects, earthworms, and slugs.

Brook salamanders may breed anytime from early spring to midsummer. After mating, females glue their eggs to the underside of rocks in the water. Several salamanders may use the same rock, each laying about 30 white or pale yellow eggs. The eggs are a little smaller than peas.

About one month later, the eggs hatch into larvae that must live in water for several weeks before changing into adults.

THREE-LINED

LONG-TAILED

TWO-LINED

41

WOODLAND SALAMANDERS

DESCRIPTION: There are many kinds of woodland salamanders, but two of the most common are the slimy and the red-backed.

All salamanders have moist, slippery skins. But slimy salamanders are covered with a sticky goo that's difficult to wash off your hands. They are black above and speckled all over with golden or silvery-white. Throat and belly are plain gray, but the belly is slightly darker. Adults are 5 to 7 inches long from nose to tip of tail.

Red-backed salamanders are dark brown or black. A wide, straight-edged, reddish stripe runs down the back and tail. (Other woodland salamanders may have narrow or wavy stripes.) Some are not red at all. They are dark gray or black on top. These are called lead-backed salamanders.

Both red-backed and lead-backed salamanders have black and white (or yellow) flecks on belly and sides, as if they were sprinkled with salt and pepper. This is a good clue to their identities. Adults are 2 to 4 inches long.

HABITS: As their name says, these amphibians live in moist woodlands, where they can find plenty of damp hiding places. They also sometimes live in city parks, cemeteries, and empty lots. Not many types of salamanders can survive in town.

Food includes earthworms, insects, and spiders.

Females that have mated lay their eggs under stones or inside rotting logs and stay with them until they're hatched. Unlike most salamanders, their babies don't spend the first weeks of life swimming underwater. They change from larvae to tiny, air-breathing adults while still in the eggs.

RED-BACKED

SLIMY

TIGER SALAMANDERS

DESCRIPTION: Tiger salamanders have blotchy markings that look something like tiger stripes. These marks are white or yellow on a black, brown, or greenish-brown body. They cover the entire salamander, including its face and feet.

The body is plump, with a tail that is flattened from side to side. Adults are about 8 inches long from nose to tip of tail.

HABITS: These amphibians spend most of their time underground in caves or animal burrows. They usually only come to the surface after heavy spring rains. This is when they look for mates and lay eggs in ponds or quiet streams. They wander at night during the breeding season, hiding under rocks and logs during the day.

Tiger salamanders won't bite, but they are very strong. It might surprise you how easily they can wriggle out of your grasp.

When it comes to food, though, they are as ferocious as real tigers. Anything small enough to be swallowed whole is fair game, including grasshoppers, spiders, worms, and young mice.

BARRED   GRAY   CALIFORNIA   BLOTCHED

THERE ARE DIFFERENT PATTERNS ON TIGER SALAMANDERS. HERE ARE FOUR.

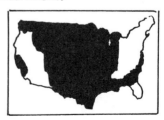

RED AND MUD SALAMANDERS

DESCRIPTION: Red salamanders, as their name says, are red or reddish-pink. Head, back, tail, and sides are speckled with tiny black spots. These markings are oddly shaped, not perfectly round. In some kinds, the back is a smoky-red color that makes it hard to see the spots. Their eyes are yellow.

Mud salamanders look very much like their red cousins, but they have brown eyes and round, or nearly round, black spots.

Both kinds are 3 to 6 inches long from nose to tip of tail when fully grown.

HABITS: Mud salamanders prefer muddy streams where the water is cloudy and the bottom soft and squishy. Reds like clear water, usually living only where the bottom is sand or gravel.

Both eat aquatic insects they find along the bottom. And both hide under stones in or near the water, or in holes along the shore.

In the fall, mated females attach their eggs to sticks, rocks, and other objects beneath the water. Each pea-sized egg hangs by a tiny stalk.

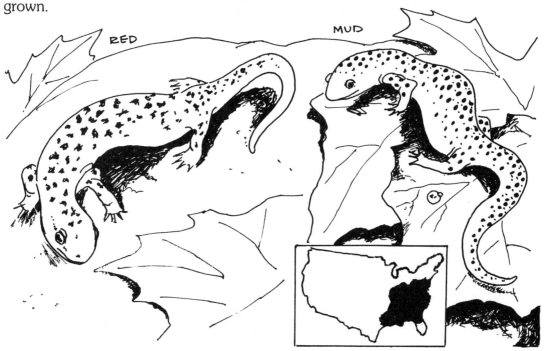

RED   MUD

TRUE TOADS

DESCRIPTION: True toads look like fat, slow-moving frogs. They have dry, warty skin. Behind each eye is a large, round or kidney-shaped lump. In bright light, the pupils of a toad's eyes are horizontal slits. And there are 2 brownish-black tubercles on the bottom of each hind foot.

General color is tan to dark brown with dark splotches, spots, or bands on back and legs. Often, a white line goes straight down the middle of the back. Males usually have black or smoky-gray throats.

True toads are often confused with spadefoot toads (p. 48). But telling them apart is easy. The spadefoot doesn't have any large lumps behind the eyes. Its pupils are vertical in bright light. And there's only one tubercle on each hind foot.

Adults are 2 to 4 inches long, not including their legs.

HABITS: These chubby hunters hide by day and hunt by night. Seemingly always hungry, they will gobble down just about any animal they can stuff into their huge mouths.

Toads don't bite and they can't give you warts. But you should *always* wash your hands after touching them. The lumps on their bodies, including the ones behind each eye, secrete poison onto their skin.

This poison causes a burning sensation in the mouths of most predators. After one taste, a predator may never sample toads again, even if very hungry. About the only animals not affected are snakes and turtles. But the poison can make you very uncomfortable if it gets into your eyes or mouth.

Toads lay strings of black eggs in ponds, ditches, and other quiet waters after heavy rains. During droughts, when it's very hot and dry, they burrow underground and sleep for weeks or months until the next downpour.

THERE ARE
TWO
TUBERCLES
ON
BOTTOM OF
FOOT

SPADEFOOT TOADS

DESCRIPTION: Spadefoot toads, chubby and slow-moving, are about 1½ to 3 inches long from nose to rump. They resemble true toads (p. 46) but the two can easily be told apart.

Spadefoots don't have large, lumpy poison glands like the ones behind a true toad's eyes. In bright light, their pupils are vertical ovals. (A true toad has horizontal pupils.) And there is only one tubercle on the bottom of a spadefoot's hind feet, instead of two, as with true toads.

These amphibians are drab gray, yellow, or brown. Often they are covered with a network of dark, wavy lines. Males have dark throats.

HABITS: The name "spadefoot" comes from the way these toads use their tubercles as tiny garden spades. They can dig backward into the ground or under a heavy rock just by shuffling their feet. Come nighttime, they hop out to hunt for insects and spiders.

If it's too hot or dry, spadefoots can stay underground for months until it rains. A protective cocoon of dead skin forms around them to prevent drying out.

These animals have a bitter-tasting skin poison that discourages most predators. It isn't dangerous to hu-

mans, but it can cause a painful burning sensation if it gets into your eyes or mouth. Always wash up after touching toads.

Many spadefoot toads live where it is dry much of the year. After a heavy rain storm, adults gather in pools of water to breed. Females glue sausage-like clusters of eggs to underwater plants. The tadpoles hatch in a day or two and race to mature into adults before the sun dries up their home, killing them.

If the water level becomes dangerously low, they may gather into a school and fan the bottom with their tails. This blows mud out of the way, forming a shallow hole where the water is deeper. This trick can give the baby toads just enough extra time to become land-loving adults before the water evaporates completely.

TOADS MOVE FEET BACK AND FORTH TO DIG BURROWS.

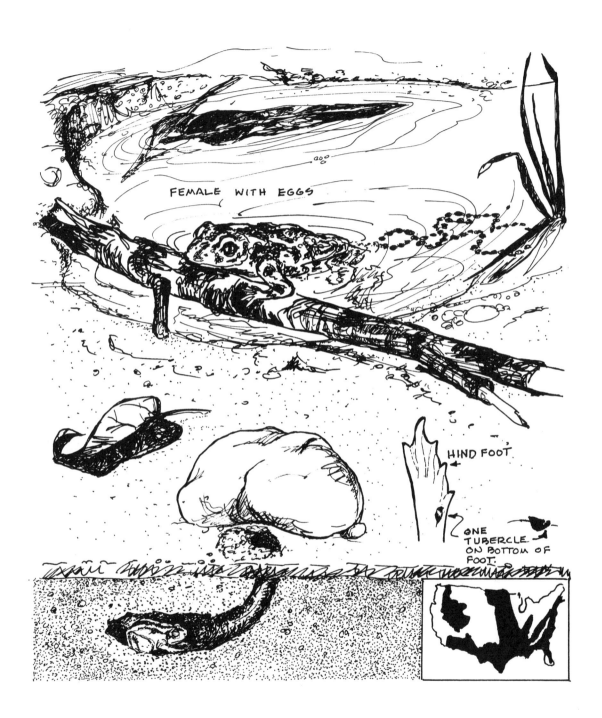

FEMALE WITH EGGS

HIND FOOT

ONE
TUBERCLE
ON BOTTOM OF
FOOT.

NARROW-MOUTH TOADS

DESCRIPTION: Narrow-mouth toads are among the strangest amphibians you might meet under a rock. They are easily identified by their pointy snouts and the fold of skin that looks like a shirt collar behind their heads. Narrow-mouths aren't dry and warty like other toads. Their skin is smooth and moist. Adults are about 1½ inches long from snout to rump.

There are two types of narrow-mouths. The Great Plains type is gray, light tan, or olive green with practically no markings. Its belly is plain white.

The eastern narrow-mouth is the same general color, but is covered with dark spots and squiggles. Its belly is so thick with them that only a little white shows through.

Both kinds change color depending on the temperature and how active they are. Males have dark throats.

HABITS: The shy narrow-mouth toad rarely comes out except to search for food at night. They eat almost nothing but ants, using their pointy snouts as shovels to dig them up. Their thick skin protects them from bites, and if a few ants manage to reach a narrow-mouth's eyes—ZIP! The fold of skin behind its head comes forward and wipes them away!

These toads breed in large pools of water that form after heavy rains in spring and summer. Females can lay more than 800 eggs in one night. The eggs hatch in only two days and the tadpoles become adults in 20 to 30 days more.

Narrow-mouths have a mild poison in their moist skin that keeps most predators from eating them. It can cause a burning sensation if it gets in your mouth or eyes. Always wash your hands after handling one of these toads.

NARROW-MOUTHS ARE VERY SMALL

GREAT PLAINS

EASTERN

THIS IS A VERY SMALL TOAD - 1"-1½"

Reptiles

SKINKS

DESCRIPTION: Skinks are hot-dog-shaped lizards with short legs and long tails. Their smooth scales give them a polished appearance.

Most are some shade of brown with several lighter and darker stripes on body and tail. They usually have a wide, dark brown band on each side, from the eyes to nearly the tips of their tails.

Five-lined skinks are very common. Females and young have 5 dirty white stripes. In adult males, these markings fade until they are barely visible. The young have bright blue tails, but this color also fades as they grow older. During the spring breeding season, males become reddish-orange on their jaws.

The Great Plains skink has only a hint of stripes. Adults are light tan or gray and most of their scales have black or brown edges. The scales on a Great Plains's sides are arranged in diagonal rows. In all other skinks, they are in horizontal rows. The young of this lizard are solid black with blue tails, and orange and white spots on the head.

Striped varieties, including the five-lined skink, are 5 to 8 inches long from nose to tail-tip. Great Plains are up to 13 inches long.

Racerunner lizards (p. 58) might be confused with skinks, but their belly scales are much larger than the tiny scales on their backs. Skinks have scales that are all about the same size. Some skinks, however, do have a row of larger scales under the tail but not on the belly.

HABITS: Skinks are fast, nervous reptiles. They hunt by day and hide by night. Food is usually insects and other arthropods.

They almost always bite when caught and large ones can pinch painfully. Skinks can purposely break off parts of their long tails when frightened. The pieces attract attention by wiggling wildly so the owners can escape unnoticed. A new tail always grows back but it is never as long or as pretty as the original.

All skinks in the United States lay eggs. In a few kinds, the female constantly turns them to prevent mold from growing where they touch the damp soil.

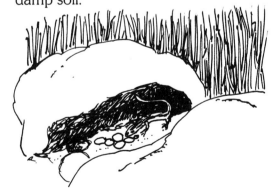

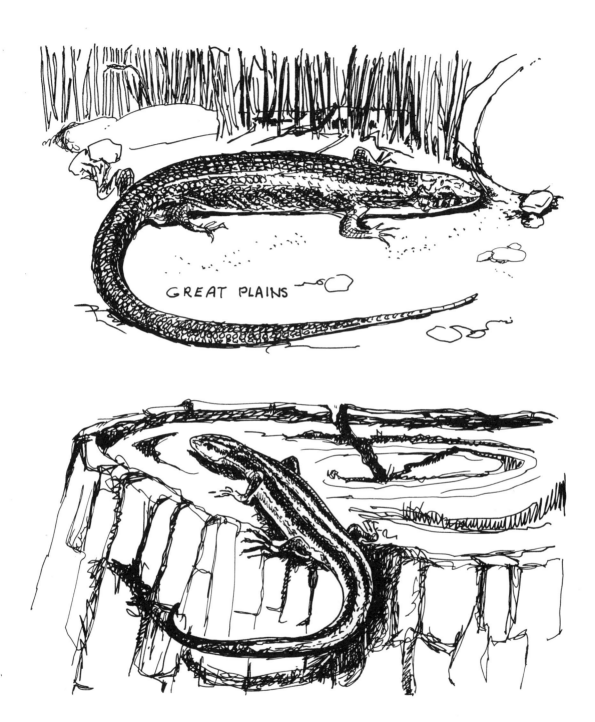

GREAT PLAINS

COLLARED LIZARDS

DESCRIPTION: The collared lizard got its name from 2 black stripes around its neck that look like a shirt collar. These chubby animals have flat, wide heads that seem too large for their bodies. Adults are 8 to 12 inches long with skinny tails that take up more than half of this length.

Legs and tail are light green, blue, brown, or yellow. The back is darker, sprinkled with light spots. Very old individuals may be the same color all over, but they always have their collars.

Males sometimes have a tinge of orange on their throats. Orange spots or bars decorate the sides of females carrying eggs inside their bodies.

HABITS: These reptiles are hard to catch because they are so fast. If one is hiding under a rock that you turn over, chances are it will take off at full speed and head for another rock. It may even rise up on its hind legs as it runs, looking for all the world like a tiny dinosaur.

Collared lizards aren't dangerous, but they do have strong jaws, sharp teeth, and bad tempers. They always try to bite, and even small ones can nip painfully.

These reptiles like to sun themselves on rocks and gobble up insects that wander by. They also eat other reptiles, including smaller collared lizards.

Males stake out territories and chase away other males that enter their tiny kingdoms. One territory covers about as much ground as a house.

Females that have mated lay 4 to 24 grape-sized eggs in loose sand or under large rocks. The eggs hatch in late summer or early fall.

HORNED LIZARDS

DESCRIPTION: Horned lizards are covered all over with short, fleshy spines. Longer and stiffer spines stick out from the back of their flat heads, like braids of hair. Their wide, flat bodies end in a stubby tail.

General color is yellowish-brown to reddish-brown with two rows of dark blotches down the back. Adults are 2½ to 4 inches long from nose to tip of tail. Young look like their parents, but are about 1½ inches long at hatching.

HABITS: These odd reptiles seem to love the heat. They can stand temperatures that would kill most other American lizards. On cool or overcast days, they often remain hidden under rocks or in animal burrows.

When they do come out, it's usually to look for ants, practically their only food. This unusual diet makes them hard to keep as pets, even though horned lizards are often sold in pet shops.

You might think these thorny creatures are safe from attack. Actually, their spines aren't very sharp and do not always keep away hungry hawks, roadrunners, or snakes.

Instead, horned lizards try to hide from predators by changing color to blend in with the ground. If that doesn't work, they can scamper away surprisingly fast on their short legs. When picked up, many inflate themselves with air so they'll be more difficult to swallow.

Females that have mated lay about 20 small eggs beneath stones or in sandy soil. The eggs hatch in late summer. Some kinds give birth to live young, whose soft spines harden after a few hours.

RACERUNNERS

DESCRIPTION: Racerunners are thin, striped lizards with long tails. Adults are 6 to 9 inches long, and more than half of this length is tail. Young are only 1 to 1½ inches long at hatching.

Racerunners are covered with thousands of tiny scales about the size of sand grains. This makes them feel slightly rough. But they have 8 rows of much larger, rectangular scales on the belly.

These lizards come in two varieties. The six-lined racerunner has 6 yellow, white, pale gray, or pale blue stripes on a dark brown body and tail. The prairie racerunner has seven lines on a green body. Its tail and legs are brown.

Males of both kinds have light blue bellies. Young have blue tails.

Skinks (p. 54) are sometimes confused with racerunners. But like most lizards, a skink's belly scales are the same size as those on its back.

HABITS: Racerunners only spend nights underneath rocks and boards. Look for them in late evening or early morning, when they are cold and slow. After the sun rises and warms them up, they spend the day nervously zipping across the ground. It's impossible to capture one then.

Food is mostly insects, spiders, and scorpions.

Mating occurs in spring. In summer, females that have mated lay several clutches of eggs. The 2 to 6 white eggs are buried a few inches deep in sandy soil.

FENCE LIZARDS

DESCRIPTION: Fence lizards got their name because they often cling to trees or wooden fenceposts. The sharply pointed, keeled scales covering their backs and long tails give them another name, spiny lizards. Adults are 3 to 7 inches long from nose to tailtip.

These reptiles are drab gray or brown. Adult males are unmarked on top but have a large greenish-blue patch on either side of belly and throat. Females and young have similar but very faint decorations, or none at all. Females also have dark, wavy lines, bars, or crescent moon shapes on their backs. Both sexes often show a bit of orange or yellow on the underside of their rear legs and tails.

Side-blotched lizards (p. 60) may be confused with young or female fence lizards. Check the throat. Fence lizards have a fold of skin on either side but not in the middle. Side-blotched lizards have a fold of skin that goes all the way across the throat.

HABITS: Males use their bright blue patches to attract females. During mating season, they do "push-ups" to expose their throats and bellies for nearby females to admire. Successful males win mates. Some even keep small harems of two or three females, which they guard against rival males.

Eggs are laid in the ground in spring and hatch after about two months.

The speedy fence lizards are difficult to catch before they dart down a rodent burrow or up a tree. Hunt for them early in the morning or late in the evening, when they have cooled off.

They eat spiders, millipedes, snails, and insects of all kinds.

LOOK FOR THIS FOLD OF SKIN ON THROAT

SIDE-BLOTCHED LIZARDS

DESCRIPTION: Side-blotched lizards are 4 to 6 inches long from nose to tip of tail. The tail is as long or longer than the head and body together. Just behind each front leg is a bold, black spot.

These lizards are generally brown with straw yellow spots and stripes across their bodies, legs, and tails. Females have a light line from each eye to the base of their tails. Males have pale blue or blue-gray on throat, lower sides of body, and tail. Both sexes are speckled blue across the back.

The fence lizard (p. 59) is similar to the side-blotched. But fence lizards don't have a black spot on each side or any blue on their backs and tails. Also, the side-blotched has a fold of skin across its throat. Fence lizards have a fold on either side, but not in the middle.

HABITS: These little reptiles prefer living in dry, open areas. They are abundant in the southwest portion of the United States.

Side-blotched lizards eat mostly insects, ticks, and scorpions.

Females that have mated lay 3 to 5 eggs in the spring or summer. Sometimes they lay more than one clutch of eggs. Very few of the babies survive more than one year before they are eaten by hungry predators.

SKIN FOLD ON THROAT

EARTH SNAKES

DESCRIPTION: The little earth snakes are difficult to identify. They are gray, brown, or reddish-brown and usually unmarked. The belly is plain white, gray, or yellow. Some have a very faint light stripe down the middle of the back. There may also be a tiny light stripe on many of the body scales.

The most certain way to identify them is to look for a scale that touches the eye and the first scale behind the nostril, as pictured.

The anal scale is *usually* divided. Scales on the front half of the body are not keeled. On the back half, they are slightly keeled.

Adults are about 10 inches long.

Babies are about 4 inches long at birth.

HABITS: This is one of the few snakes that can survive in towns and cities. It is so good at hiding, however, that most people never know it's around. Earth snakes spend most of their time underground, hunting worms and soft-bodied insects. After heavy rains, they often come to the surface to lie beneath sun-warmed rocks.

Females that have found mates give birth to about five young in summer or fall. Come winter, earth snakes often curl up for a long sleep with other kinds of snakes deep in the soil.

LOOK FOR THIS SCALE

AND FOR THE DIVIDED ANAL SCALE

BROWN SNAKES AND RED-BELLIED SNAKES

DESCRIPTION: Brown snakes and red-bellied snakes are closely related. Adults are about 10 inches long. Young are 2 to 4 inches long at hatching. Anal scale is divided and body scales are keeled.

Brown snakes are gray, brown, or reddish-brown. The middle of the back is almost always lighter than the sides. There is a row of dark spots on each side of the backbone, but these may be hard to see unless the skin is stretched. In some brown snakes, the dots are connected to form a ladder pattern.

Young brown snakes have a yellowish collar that might get them mistaken for ringneck snakes (p. 66). Ringnecks, however, have smooth scales.

Red-bellied snakes are normally brown or gray on top with three pale spots on the back of the neck. There may be a wide, light stripe down the middle of the back. Or four narrow, dark stripes. Or both. They usually have bright red, unmarked bellies.

A look alike of the red-bellied is Kirtland's snake (p. 70), which also has a red underside. But a row of round, black spots along each side of this snake's belly will clear up any confusion.

HABITS: Brown snakes, like many small serpents, don't seem to mind living in big cities. They often turn up in parks and empty lots, where they hide under boards and trash. The red-bellied is more often found in the country, where there is less pollution.

Both snakes are active during the day in spring and fall. But in summer, they escape the heat by hunting at night. They mainly eat slugs and earthworms.

Instead of laying eggs, females that have mated give birth to as many as 30 babies.

LIGHT SPOTS →

BROWN
SNAKE

RED-BELLIED SNAKE

RACER SNAKES

DESCRIPTION: The snakes known as racers have slender necks, broad heads, and large brown or amber eyes. Their scales are smooth and satiny. Anal scale is divided.

Three kinds of racers are commonly found under stones and other ground cover.

Northern black racers are shiny black above and below, without any markings. There is usually some white on the chin and throat. Some rat snakes (p. 78) are black, too, but they have white bellies and keeled scales.

Blue racers are some shade of blue all over. The back is darker than the belly. Again, no markings, but chin and throat are white.

Buttermilk racers are black, blue, or olive green with light speckles. These spots may be white, yellow, tan, or pale blue. There can be a little or a lot of speckling.

Young racers all look alike. They are gray or blue-gray with a row of dark gray or reddish-brown blotches along the back. Their sides and bellies are decorated with dark, oddly shaped spots. Their tails are one solid color, without any pattern.

HABITS: Racers are the fastest snakes known. Top speed is about 3½ miles an hour. A person can easily walk faster than this on a road. But in the weedy, bushy areas these snakes call home, racers are difficult to catch.

If you should corner one, watch out! They bite viciously and thrash around when picked up. Wear gloves or you'll get scratched by their sharp teeth.

In late spring and early summer, mated females lay as many as 40 eggs beneath stones and logs or in the tunnels of small animals such as moles. The leathery white eggs hatch after two or three months.

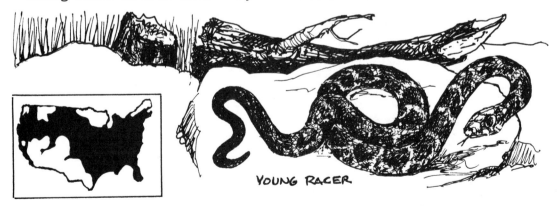

YOUNG RACER

SCARLET SNAKES

DESCRIPTION: The scarlet snake is yellow with a pointed red snout and a row of red patches along its back. Each patch is surrounded by a black border. The snake's yellowish-white belly is unmarked. Its scales are smooth and the anal scale is undivided.

Adults are 1 to 1½ feet long. Young, which look like their parents, are about 5 inches long at hatching.

Some of the colorful milk and kingsnakes (p. 76) might be mistaken for a scarlet snake. But none of these lookalikes has both a red snout *and* a belly without any pattern. Another reptile that might cause confusion is the poisonous coral snake (p. 88). In these animals, the yellow and red markings are not separated by black. If you live in coral snake country, stay away from any snake that looks like one.

HABITS: The shy scarlet snake prefers to stay under cover during the day. It comes out after dark to hunt for mice, lizards, small snakes, and reptile eggs. Scarlet snakes squeeze their prey to death before swallowing it.

After mating, females lay about 8 eggs during summer.

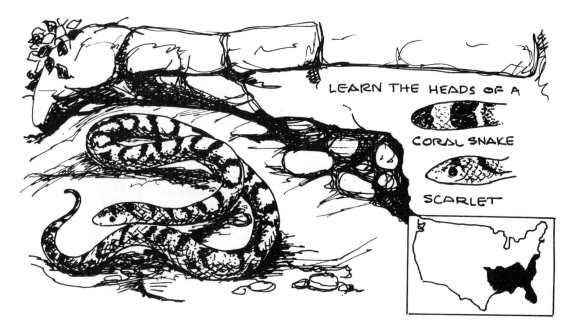

LEARN THE HEADS OF A

CORAL SNAKE

SCARLET

RINGNECK SNAKES

DESCRIPTION: Ringneck snakes are shiny black, brown, or gray with a ring of gold around their necks. Their yellow or orange bellies are spotted with black. The pattern of spots (see picture at right) will tell you what kind of ringneck you've found. In some kinds, the belly color turns to red underneath the tail.

Young brown snakes (p. 62) have a light collar that might get them mistaken for ringnecks. But brown snakes have keeled scales. Ringnecks' scales are smooth.

Adults are 10 inches to 1½ feet long. Babies are about 5 inches long when they hatch out.

HABITS: Ringnecks hide during the day and hunt at night for earthworms, salamanders, frogs, and small snakes. Sometimes a group of them can be found coiled together under the same rock. No one is sure why they do this, but it is unusual behavior for snakes.

Ringnecks are completely harmless. Instead of biting when captured, they'll use their tails to smear a smelly, white paste on your hand. Those with red under their tails often twist them around to show off this color. This trick might frighten away some predators because many brightly colored animals taste bad.

Females that have mated lay 1 to 8 eggs in underground nests. The eggs hatch in summer.

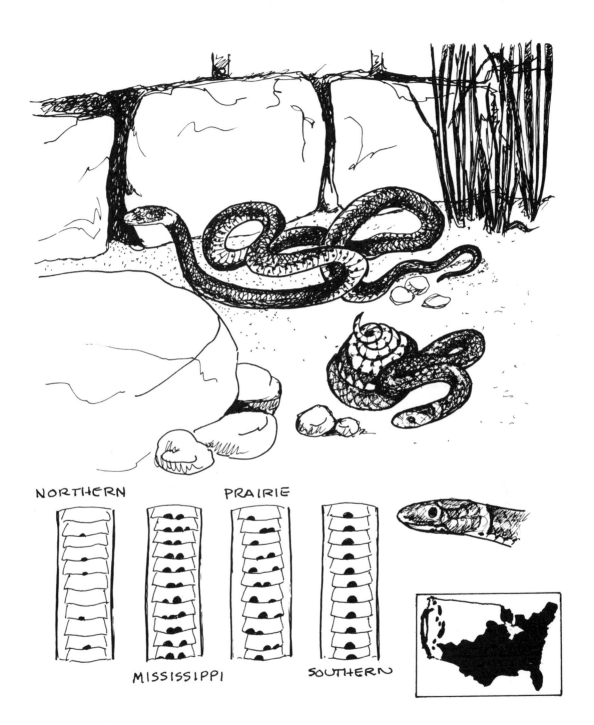

NORTHERN   PRAIRIE

MISSISSIPPI   SOUTHERN

LINED SNAKES AND GARTER SNAKES

DESCRIPTION: Almost any snake with 3 stripes—one down the middle of its back and one on each side—will be either a garter or a lined snake. Both have keeled scales and a dull, dusty appearance.

Lined snakes are easy to identify. Look for an undivided anal scale and a double row of bold, black half-moons down the yellowish or white belly. These reptiles are gray or brown on top with three gray, white, or yellow stripes. Adults are 10 inches to 1½ feet long. Babies are about 4 inches long at birth.

Garter snakes are usually dark green or reddish-brown, often with squarish black spots between their stripes. The middle stripe may be white, yellow, green, orange, or red. The side stripes are often faint and hard to see. Most garters have 2 small yellow or white spots on top of their heads. Adults average 2 feet long. Newly born garter snakes are about 8 inches long.

Most other striped snakes have 4 lines. Rosy boas (p. 82) do have 3 wide, dark brown stripes, but their shiny scales are not keeled.

HABITS: These reptiles often live under pieces of trash in empty lots, city parks, and cemeteries.

Lined snakes come out at night to hunt for earthworms. Garter snakes (named for the striped, elastic garters men used to wear to hold up their socks) search for frogs, salamanders, tadpoles, small fish, and worms during the day.

Garter snakes are bad-tempered, thrashing their tails and biting when first captured. However, they are not dangerous. The harmless lined snakes are much gentler. They don't bite or make any real attempt to escape when picked up.

Both give birth to live young. Lined snakes rarely have more than a dozen babies, but garter snakes can have more than 80!

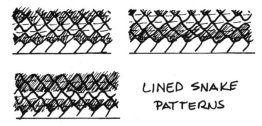

LINED SNAKE
PATTERNS

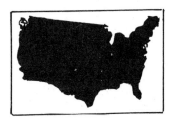

LINED SNAKE

GARTER SNAKE

KIRTLAND'S SNAKES

DESCRIPTION: The small Kirtland's snake is easy to identify when you turn it over. Look for a reddish belly with a row of round black spots along each edge. Chin and throat are yellowish. It is rusty brown on top, with 4 rows of small black spots along the back. These markings might be hard to see unless the skin is stretched, as when the snake has eaten a big meal. Scales are keeled, anal scale divided.

Adults are 1 to 1½ feet long. Young resemble adults and are about 6 inches long at birth.

A lookalike is the red-bellied snake (p. 62). But it doesn't have spots on either its belly or back.

HABITS: Like its relatives the garter snakes (p. 68), Kirtland's snake often flattens its body when disturbed. It is so good at this that some individuals seem to make themselves as flat as ribbons. They often freeze in this position until touched. Then they suddenly come alive and try to escape.

This shy reptile remains hidden most of its life. Kirtland's snake likes damp areas where its favorite foods, slugs and earthworms, are plentiful.

As many as 22 young are born alive. Babies and adults probably sleep through the winter by burrowing into soft mud.

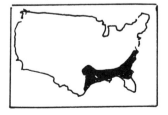

NIGHT SNAKES

DESCRIPTION: Night snakes are gray or grayish-tan with a row of large, dark gray or brown blotches down the back, and 2 or 3 rows of smaller spots on each side. The best way to identify them is by the 2 or 3 very large dark patches on the neck. These markings are connected to each eye by a wide dark stripe.

In addition, the night snake's clean white upper lip stands out clearly. Belly is yellowish or white without any pattern.

Scales are smooth. The anal scale is divided. The pupil is a vertical slit in bright light. Adults measure about $1\frac{1}{2}$ feet long. Young are about 6 inches long at hatching.

Young racers (p. 64) look like adult night snakes except that they have round pupils.

HABITS: As the name suggests, night snakes prefer to come out at night. They prowl around for small lizards and frogs. Night snakes have a very mild poison that is harmless to humans but deadly to the small animals they eat. Unlike most poisonous snakes, they have short fangs at the rear of their mouths instead of at the front.

Females that have mated lay 2 to 6 eggs in the summer. These hatch in about two months.

COACHWHIP SNAKES

DESCRIPTION: Coachwhip snakes are slender, with narrow necks, wide heads, and big eyes. The arrangement of their scales makes them look like braided leather whips. Scales are smooth. Anal scale is divided. Adults may grow to be 6 feet long.

There are two kinds of coachwhips. The eastern variety is the only snake in the United States that is black or dark brown up front and light brown toward the tail. But where one tone begins and the other ends will vary from snake to snake. Belly color always matches that of the back.

Some eastern coachwhips are solid black with red along the sides of their tails. These may be confused with northern black racers (p. 64) but racers don't have any red markings.

Western coachwhips are light yellow-brown to dark brown all over. This color doesn't change from end to end. But often there are narrow, dark crossbands on the neck, which gradually fade along the back. Belly is whitish.

Young of both kinds are light brown with narrow, dark crossbands on the front part of their bodies. A baby coachwhip's head is often darker than its back.

HABITS: Coachwhips are active during the day, even in the middle of summer, when most snakes take shelter from the heat. Look for them early in the morning, while they are still hiding, before the sun warms them up.

They move quickly and are difficult to catch. Unlike most snakes, coachwhips may actually come at you if cornered. They will bite when picked up, but are not the least bit poisonous. They may also wiggle out of your grasp by lashing their long tails back and forth.

When not resting, these snakes are constantly on the lookout for insects, rodents, snakes, lizards, small birds, and bird eggs. They swallow their prey while it's alive and (sometimes) kicking.

Mated females can lay as many as two dozen eggs during summer. The white, oblong eggs, which hatch in the fall, are coated with tiny bumps that look like grains of salt.

YOUNG COACHWHIP

WORM SNAKES

DESCRIPTION: Worm snakes are easy to identify by their two-tone color pattern. Look for plain black or dark gray on top and pink below. The belly color extends onto the sides. There are no markings of any kind.

Worm snakes have pointy heads, smooth scales, and divided anal scales. Adults are about 11 inches long. Young are about 4 inches long at hatching.

HABITS: These burrowing snakes rarely come to the surface, so finding one is a real achievement. They spend a lot of time underground because this is where they find their favorite food, earthworms. In hot weather, they tunnel deep into the soil until it cools off.

Worm snakes are completely harmless. If you're lucky enough to find one, you may notice it has a spine at the end of its tail. Don't worry. This is not a stinger and it cannot hurt you.

Females that have mated lay only 2 or 3 tiny eggs in an underground nest. These hatch in late summer.

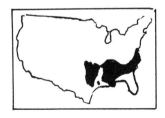

FLATHEAD AND BLACKHEAD SNAKES

DESCRIPTION: Flathead and black-head snakes all have dark brown or black heads, as if they had been dipped in ink. Many have a white collar behind their heads, followed by a black band or a row of black spots. Their bodies are plain, shiny brown above with pink, yellow, or reddish-orange bellies.

Adults are 7 to 10 inches long. Anal scale is divided. Body scales are smooth.

HABITS: Like many small, burrowing snakes, these reptiles often come to the surface after spring rains force them out of the ground.

They eat centipedes, millipedes, spiders, and small insects.

In summer, mated females lay 1 to 4 eggs, which hatch in autumn.

FLATHEAD

BLACKHEAD

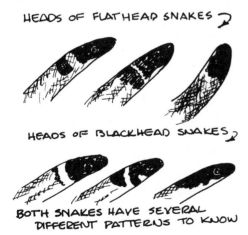

HEADS OF FLATHEAD SNAKES

HEADS OF BLACKHEAD SNAKES

BOTH SNAKES HAVE SEVERAL DIFFERENT PATTERNS TO KNOW

75

KINGSNAKES AND MILK SNAKES

DESCRIPTION: Although closely related, kingsnakes and milk snakes look very different. All have smooth, shiny scales and undivided anal scales. Adults are 3 to 4 feet long. Young have patterns similar to their parents'. They are about 1 foot long at hatching.

Kingsnakes are black or dark brown with tiny white or yellow spots on *some* of their scales. Sometimes these speckles are connected to form a chainlike pattern. An exception to this is the prairie kingsnake. This light tan reptile has one row of large brown or reddish-brown blotches down its back and two rows of smaller blotches on each side.

Milk snakes are banded with red on a white or yellow background. Some have brown blotches instead of bands. But all milk snakes have markings that are surrounded by narrow black borders.

A few kinds of rat snakes (p. 78) and racers (p. 64) are patterned like milk and kingsnakes. But these lookalikes have divided anal scales. Some kinds of milk snakes closely resemble poisonous coral snakes (p. 88). In coral snakes, however, the red and yellow touch. In all harmless serpents, black separates these colors. If in doubt, leave the snake alone.

HABITS: Milk snakes get their name from an old belief that they suck milk from cows at night. This isn't true, but they do search for food around barns and other farm buildings where cows might be kept.

Both milk and kingsnakes eat lizards, rodents, small birds, bird eggs, and turtle eggs. But they are best known for eating other snakes, including their own kinds. Not even rattlers are safe, because milk and kingsnakes are not affected by their poison. Prey is constricted, or squeezed to death, before being swallowed.

In summer, females that have mated lay about 10 eggs that hatch by autumn.

PRAIRIE KINGSNAKE   MILK SNAKE   CORAL SNAKE

KNOW THESE PATTERNS!

76

KINGSNAKE

MILK SNAKE

77

RAT SNAKES

DESCRIPTION: Rat snakes come in many color patterns, but one thing they all have in common is shape. In cross section, they are shaped like a piece of bread. Look for a sharp angle where the flat belly and sides meet. Most other snakes are round like a garden hose.

Adults have weakly keeled scales on their backs. They are smooth everywhere else. Very young rat snakes are smooth all over. The anal scale is divided.

Rat snakes hatch with one row of large blotches down the back and two or three rows of smaller spots on each side. These gray, brown, or reddish-brown markings are on a background of light gray or light brown.

This pattern is the one that most rat snakes will have for life. But black rats and yellow rats slowly change color as they grow older. The first one turns solid black with a white belly. The other becomes yellow with four brown stripes.

Young are easily confused with baby racers (p. 64). Racers, however, only have a faint pattern, or none at all, on their tails. Rat snakes are boldly marked right to the tip of their tails.

Babies are 10 inches to 1½ feet at hatching. Full-grown snakes are 4 to 6 feet long.

HABITS: Rat snakes got their name because they eat mostly mice and rats. Baby rabbits, small birds, bird eggs, lizards, and frogs are also on their list of favorite foods. These reptiles are constrictors. That is, they squeeze their prey to death before swallowing it.

Rat snakes spend most of their time on the ground, but they are excellent climbers. By wedging the sharp edges of their bellies into cracks in the bark, they can crawl up the side of a tree without holding onto any branches.

While they aren't poisonous, rat snakes can seem awfully dangerous when cornered—vibrating their tails, hissing loudly, and striking. They may bite when picked up. If you aren't wearing gloves, you might get scratched by their sharp teeth.

Rat snakes lay 12 to 24 leathery white eggs in spring or summer.

RAT SNAKES HATCHING

YELLOW RAT SNAKE

GREAT PLAINS RAT SNAKE

← ANAL SCALE

LOOK FOR THIS PATTERN UNDER YOUNG RAT SNAKES' TAILS

LOOK FOR THIS SHAPE

RAT SNAKE   OTHER SNAKES

HOGNOSE SNAKES

DESCRIPTION: The hognose snake is well named. A wide scale at the end of its snout curves out and up, like a pig's nose.

This thick-bodied reptile is so fat it doesn't appear to have any neck. Body scales are keeled, including the one on the snout. The anal scale is divided.

Hognoses are usually yellow, gray, or brown, with dark brown or black blotches on back and tail. Some individuals are black all over. Most have a wide, dark stripe that looks like a mask across the face. There is usually a large dark patch on each side of the neck.

Adults are 1½ to 2 feet long. Babies are about 6 inches long at hatching and look like their parents.

HABITS: Because of the way they act when frightened, hognose snakes are also called spread heads, blow snakes, and spreading adders. Most flatten their heads and spread their necks to the sides when cornered. They also hiss loudly and strike. If that fails to scare away an enemy, many will roll over and play dead. Turn them right side up and they roll over again!

The hognose uses its upturned snout as a shovel for digging up the toads, lizards, snakes, and reptile eggs it eats.

Mated females lay 10 to 20 eggs in sandy soil during midsummer. The eggs hatch by autumn.

BULLSNAKES

DESCRIPTION: Once you've met a bullsnake, you'll never forget what one looks like.

These reptiles have pointy, bullet-shaped heads that are so narrow it's hard to tell where the neck begins. They are yellow with black, brown, or reddish-brown blotches. On the tail, these blotches become bands that give bullsnakes a kind of ring-tailed appearance. Markings at both ends of the body are darker than those in the middle. No other snake's pattern is like this.

Strongly keeled scales make bullsnakes feel as rough as sandpaper. The anal scale is undivided. Adults are 4 to 6 feet long. Babies are about 1 foot long at hatching and look just like their parents.

HABITS: "The snake with a slow leak" is a good way to describe this one. If cornered, they rear back with their heads off the ground, hissing wildly. Bullsnakes can hiss while breathing in and out, so the noise is continuous. They sound like leaking bicycle tires.

They can give you a good bite, but bulls aren't poisonous, and are dangerous only to mice, rats, and baby rabbits. A single snake can save a farmer hundreds of dollars in one year by eating rodents that would otherwise attack crops and stored food. Bullsnakes kill by constriction. That is, they squeeze their prey until it stops breathing.

In summer, mated females lay about one dozen eggs under logs and large rocks. The eggs, which stick together in a clump, hatch in early fall.

TOP OF HEAD

RUBBER AND ROSY BOAS

DESCRIPTION: The only relatives of the boa constrictor in all of North America are the rubber and rosy boas.

These heavy-bodied snakes have small heads and smooth, glossy scales. The pupils of their eyes are vertical slits. Unlike most snakes, they have narrow belly scales that don't completely cover their undersides. Males always have a bony spur or claw on each side of the undivided anal scale. Females usually don't have these.

The rubber boa looks and feels like rubber. It is plain, dark brown above with a pale yellow belly. Young may be pink or light brown on top. The narrow head is easily mistaken for the short, blunt tail. Adults are 1½ to 2½ feet long. Babies measure about 10 inches long at birth.

Rosy boas are dirty white, gray, or rose colored with three wide, brown stripes. Sometimes the stripes are broken into spots and blotches. The belly is white with gray spots. Young are about 1 foot long at birth and resemble the 2- to 4-foot-long adults.

HABITS: These slow-moving snakes are completely safe to handle. They seem never to bite. Instead, they often roll into a ball when frightened. With its head safely hidden in the center, a boa then waves its blunt tail back and forth.

Predators are usually fooled into thinking this is the real head, biting it without doing the snake much harm. Rubber boas are so good at this trick they are nicknamed the two-headed snake.

Both kinds of boas stay under cover during the day. At night, they go hunting for lizards, mice, and small birds. Prey is constricted, or squeezed to death, before it is swallowed.

Females that have mated give birth to fewer than 10 live babies.

ROSY BOA

RUBBER BOA

RUBBER BOA
HEAD

ROSY BOA
HEAD

SMALL
SPUR

ON SIDE OF BODY ABOVE ANAL SCALE

RATTLESNAKES

DESCRIPTION: Be *very* careful if you find a rattlesnake. These animals are dangerously poisonous.

The papery, grayish-brown rattles on their tails are a good way to recognize them. These look like stacks of doughnuts flattened from side to side. Even if the delicate rattles all break off, there will still be a knob left on the snake's tail. Harmless snakes all have tails that taper to a point, except for rubber boas (p. 82).

Unfortunately, all of the other poisonous snakes of the United States have tapering tails, too—the copperheads and cottonmouths (p. 86) and coral snakes (p. 88).

A rattlesnake's tail and rattles are much narrower than its body. Like their copperhead cousins, they have a deep pit between eye and nostril, and the pupils of their eyes are vertical slits.

Rattlers come in grays, yellows, and browns. They are marked with large, dark blotches, diamonds, or zigzags. In some kinds, the tail is solid black. Many have broad, yellowish-white or brownish-black stripes on their faces.

Babies are about 10 inches long at birth. Adults can be from 2 to 8 feet long, depending on the kind of snake.

HABITS: Don't ever try to get near a rattlesnake. Even babies are dangerous because they are born with fangs and a large supply of poison.

Few people ever die from rattlesnake bites. But these snakes can make a person very sick, and if you are bitten on a hand or foot, their poison can cause permanent damage. They use this poison to kill mice, small birds, frogs, lizards, and insects for food. Without it, they would starve.

The pits on their faces allow rattlesnakes to find and strike prey even in total darkness. Heat-sensitive nerves in the pits let them "see" the body heat of other animals.

Mated females give birth to about 10 live young. Each baby is born with a papery bump on the end of its tail. This is the first segment of its rattle. But you cannot tell how many birthdays a rattler's had by counting these segments. New segments are added every time a snake sheds its old skin, which is several times a year. And the last few pieces always break off as the rattle becomes too long.

Scientists believe rattlesnakes developed their rattles over millions of years as a way of warning large animals not to step on them.

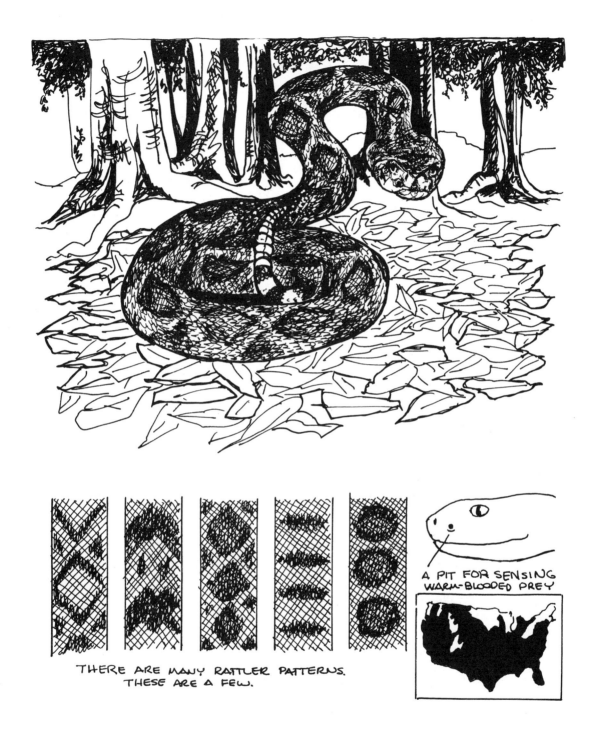

THERE ARE MANY RATTLER PATTERNS.
THESE ARE A FEW.

A PIT FOR SENSING
WARM-BLOODED PREY

COPPERHEADS AND COTTONMOUTHS

DESCRIPTION: Copperheads and cottonmouths are related to rattlesnakes (p. 84). They are just as dangerous, too, so watch out.

Three things positively identify copperheads and cottonmouths. They have a deep pit or indentation between each eye and nostril. In bright light, the pupils of their eyes are vertical slits. And, they don't have rattles on their tails.

The young of both snakes are similar. Copperheads are pinkish-tan with dark brown hourglass-shaped bands from neck to tail. The edges of these markings are darker than the centers. As their name says, copperheads usually have heads the color of a shiny new penny.

Cottonmouth babies are dark brown, including their heads and hourglass markings. A wide, dark stripe passes through each eye.

Both kinds of snakes have yellow tail-tips when young. But as they grow older, the yellow fades and eventually disappears. No other snake has this decoration.

Copperheads have the same markings throughout life. Cottonmouths lose their pattern as they mature, becoming almost solid dark brown or black.

Adults are about 4 feet long. Babies are about 10 inches at birth.

Many harmless water snakes are mistaken for adult cottonmouths. Behavior helps in telling them apart. Cottonmouths vibrate their tails when frightened. Water snakes don't. Cottonmouths stand their ground or crawl slowly away when disturbed. Water snakes zip quickly away. When cornered, a cottonmouth may open its mouth very wide to show off the snowy white lining that gives it its name. Water snakes never do this.

HABITS: Like their rattlesnake cousins, copperheads and cottonmouths use the pits on their faces to "see" in the dark. Heat-sensitive nerves in the pits detect the body heat of other animals. They can find and bite prey even in total blackness.

In daylight, the young can lure small, curious animals into striking range by wiggling their brightly-colored tails.

Food includes large insects, fish, frogs, salamanders, lizards, mice, and birds.

Young are born alive, about 10 to a litter. They have fangs and plenty of poison at birth, so *never* pick up even a small copperhead or cottonmouth.

COPPERHEAD

COTTONMOUTH

PIT

COTTONMOUTH

87

CORAL SNAKES

DESCRIPTION: *Watch out!* These brightly colored snakes are deadly poisonous. Their pattern of red, yellow, and black rings is a signal to beware. The red and yellow always touch. The snout is solid black.

Adults are 1½ to 2½ feet long. Young coral snakes, about 8 inches long when they hatch, look just like their parents.

Several harmless snakes frighten away predators by mimicking, or imitating, coral snakes. Scarlet snakes (p. 65) and some kingsnakes (p. 76) are especially good at this. But it's easy to tell the mimics from the real thing. The mimics always have black between the red and yellow. Sometimes they may have black-edge blotches instead of rings. But the red and yellow *never* touch in harmless snakes.

HABITS: Coral snakes are remarkably timid, considering how dangerous they are. They usually stay hidden, except early in the morning when hunting for lizards, frogs, and small snakes.

Their poison is extremely potent, and anyone bitten by a coral snake should get to a doctor right away. Fortunately, few people even see this shy reptile, so bites are rare.

When alarmed, some coral snakes curl their tails into a corkscrew shape and wave them overhead. They probably do this to draw attention from their heads in case a predator is foolish enough to attack.

Females that have mated lay 2 to 4 white, sausage-shaped eggs.

YELLOW AND RED TOUCH

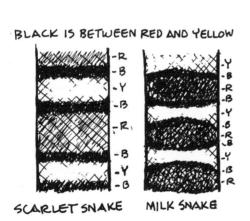

BLACK IS BETWEEN RED AND YELLOW

SCARLET SNAKE MILK SNAKE

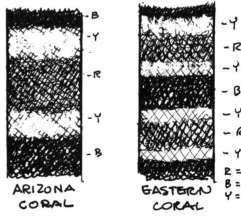

ARIZONA CORAL EASTERN CORAL

R = RED
B = BLACK
Y = YELLOW

BIBLIOGRAPHY

Arthropods

Conklin, Gladys, *The Bug Club Book,* Holiday House, New York, 1966.
Fabre, J. Henri, *Insect Adventures,* World Book Co., Yonkers, New York, 1918. Retold for children by Louise Seymour Hasbrouck.
Harpster, Hilda T., *The Insect World,* The Viking Press, New York, 1947.
Hutchins, Ross E., *The Ant Realm,* Dodd, Mead, and Co., New York, 1967.
————, *Insects—Hunters and Trappers,* Rand McNally and Co., New York, 1957.
Lutz, Frank E., *A Lot of Insects,* G. P. Putnam's Sons, New York, 1941.
Needham, James G., *Introducing Insects,* The Jaques Cattell Press, Lancaster, PA, 1940.
Patent, Dorothy Hinshaw, *Spider Magic,* Holiday House, New York, 1982.

Reptiles and Amphibians

Barker, Will, *Familiar Reptiles and Amphibians of America,* Harper and Row Publishers, New York, 1964.
Huntington, Harriet E., *Let's Look at Reptiles,* Doubleday and Co., Garden City, New York, 1973.
Morris, Percy A., *Boy's Book of Snakes,* The Ronald Press Co., New York, 1948.

OLDER READERS MIGHT FIND THE FOLLOWING FIELD GUIDES USEFUL.

Arthropods

Bland, Roger G. and H. E. Jaques, *How to Know the Insects,* William C. Brown Co., Dubuque, IA, 1978.

Borror, Donald J. and Richard E. White, *A Field Guide to the Insects of America North of Mexico,* Houghton Mifflin Co., Boston, 1970.

Reptiles and Amphibians

Conant, Roger, *A Field Guide to Reptiles and Amphibians of Eastern and Central North America,* Houghton Mifflin Co., Boston, 1975.

Schmidt, Karl P. and D. Dwight Davis, *Field Book of Snakes of the United States and Canada,* G. P. Putnam's Sons, New York, 1941.

Stebbins, Robert C., *A Field Guide to Western Reptiles and Amphibians,* Houghton Mifflin Co., Boston 1966.

INDEX

Numbers in *italics* are pages with illustrations.